ENGLISH
ROMANTIC PARTSONGS

Selected and edited by

Paul Hillier

Contents

Introduction

There are many misinformed opinions about nineteenth-century England, but some of the more regrettable ones concern music, where the use of the word 'Victorian' is still usually pejorative. In most cases any such opinion is a received one—relatively few people have actually listened to more than a few fragments of 'Victoriana', though the tendency to ridicule the style and much that its period apparently represents may seem natural to anyone performing it today. Yet if the practice of 'early music' teaches us one thing, it should be to approach the music of the past on its own terms and with reference to the cultural climate that nurtured it; that done, we may treat it simply as music to satisfy our own tastes and needs. It would not be out of place to suggest that Victorian music is now due for a revival—on its own terms—and that *we* would be the benefactors of such consideration. We would at the very least become more fully aware of our musical heritage and of how things today came to be as they are.

It is a common assumption that the rediscovery of 'early' music and the growth of societies for singing madrigals were a development of the early twentieth century, to which latterly we have added professionalism and a greatly extended repertoire as the result of exhaustive research. In fact this began in the eighteenth century (in truth it had never entirely stopped). In 1741 an amateur countertenor by the name of John Immyns, an attorney by profession, founded the Madrigal Society and

> got together a few persons who had spent their lives in the practice of psalmody . . . They were mostly mechanics; some weavers from Spitalfields, others of various trades and occupations; they met at first at the Twelve Bells, an alehouse in Bride-Lane, Fleet-Street, and Immyns was both their president and instructor; their subscription was five shillings and six-pence a quarter, which defrayed their expenses in books and music paper, and afforded them the refreshments of porter and tobacco . . .
>
> (Hawkins, *A General History . . . of Music*, London, 1776)

Nor was this the oldest musical club. Immyns's taste for 'ancient' music had no doubt been acquired through his work as copyist for Dr Pepusch's 'Academy of Ancient Music', and its activities and success were stimulated by the general interest in antiquarian pursuits that accompanied the growth of romanticism and formed a reaction to the increasing industrialization of town and country. The immediate result of such societies was an expansion of the publication of old music, which soon ranged back to the later Middle Ages, but in time the composition of new repertoire was also encouraged. In 1811 the Madrigal Society inaugurated a competition for new madrigals for which Samuel Wesley composed *O sing unto mie Roundelaie*. Although it did not win, it is a fine example of successful pastiche, complete with antiquarian spelling in its original printing.

Composition in imitation of the madrigal style continued throughout the nineteenth century; there are examples by William Beale, T. F. Walmisley, John Stainer, and Charles Wood, to name only a few. But the most significant figure in the madrigal revival, and one of England's more gifted nineteenth-century composers, was Robert Lucas Pearsall.

Pearsall was born in Bristol and studied law, though ill health cut short his career. He turned instead to music and other largely antiquarian interests, and was a founder member of the Bristol Madrigal Society (1837). He later settled abroad and purchased a castle on the shores of Lake Constance, a suitable setting for his various medieval hobbies. His partsongs, including many madrigalian compositions, form a modest but significant contribution to the English music of the period. Indeed, works such as *Lay a garland* have been paid lip-service for decades, but are still almost unknown to modern audiences. In order to stimulate some interest in an unjustly neglected minor composer one sometimes risks exaggerating his praise: Pearsall's music is often extremely attractive and in some instances deeply expressive—no more, no less, but he certainly merits our attention.

The madrigal is distinguished from the partsong by its polyphonic part-writing and generally non-chromatic harmony. The partsong itself is more harmonically conceived—indeed, at its simplest it is essentially a melody harmonized by the lower voices. Furthermore, the partsong is normally intended for performance with chorus rather than solo voices.

Another type of composition generally intended, like the madrigal, for solo voices was the Glee, a uniquely English creation which flourished in the eighteenth century as the convivial music of all-male musical societies. *Music all powerful* is a typical example of this form, with its several sections clearly defined by full cadences and a change of time signature. Although a composer such as John Goss was writing glees well into the nineteenth century, the partsong (or choral song, as it was often called) quickly established itself as more suitable for mixed-voice music-making, which was now on the increase. Composers generally wrote in several idioms and few were like William Horsley or Samuel Webbe (the latter not represented here) who were known almost exclusively as glee composers. Henry Bishop produced a vast amount of music for the stage from which much was extracted and published variously as songs, glees, and partsongs. John Hatton toured extensively as a pianist and *buffo* vocalist (including a solo tour of the USA) and composed many songs (*To Anthea, Simon the Cellarer*) and partsongs; these reveal a clear melodic gift, though his remains a minor talent at best.

More distinguished musical minds began treating the choral song as something of musical substance. A sensibility for choral texture begins to colour the partsongs of Macfarren, Benedict and Sterndale Bennett, who, taking what they would from madrigal and glee, created idiomatic compositions in a genuinely new 'Victorian' style. At the same time, the influence of Mendelssohn on English music began to be felt, an influence that was strong, long-lasting, and not universally approved of. His presence was most pronounced in the world of oratorio and instrumental composition, but his partsongs, supplied with English translations, became immensely popular (as did their originals in Germany). Mendelssohn was also acquainted with the English glee tradition and counted William Horsley among his musical friends. The German equivalent of the Glee Club, the *Liedertafel*, was founded by Mendelssohn's teacher, Karl Friedrich Zelter. But Mendelssohn himself was attempting something altogether larger, and in his partsongs headed '*Im Freien zu singen*' was keen to break free from the chamber music associations evoked by the use of voices with piano (the norm for Schubert's compositions for mixed voices).

William Sterndale Bennett is still an unduly neglected figure in the history of English music. He was a lifelong friend of Mendelssohn, who held him in high esteem, as did Schumann. Amongst his works is the sacred cantata *The Woman of Samaria*, with its well-known quartet 'God is a spirit', some very fine piano music (including four concertos), and a number of attractive songs. The influence of Mendelssohn is undeniable, though hardly a reason for ignoring one of the few nineteenth-century English composers who was widely admired abroad. Bennett's influence on English musical life has also not been fully appreciated—he produced the first English language edition of the *St Matthew Passion*, was director of the (now Royal) Philharmonic Society, founded the Bach Society (now the Bach Choir), and was Principal of the Royal Academy of Music.

The exchange of music and musicians between England and Germany was a strong feature of the nineteenth century—England being regarded primarily as an important market for performers, while Germany perhaps enjoying the greater prestige for its composers. But Hugo Pierson, potentially one of England's most significant *lied* composers, emigrated to Germany, so the exchange was in both directions. Julius Benedict moved the opposite way. He was born in Stuttgart and studied under Weber, later publishing a study of his mentor. He eventually settled in England, became a British subject, and was even knighted in 1871. His most famous work was the opera *The Lily of Killarney*, produced in London in 1862, from which we still hear the popular duet 'The moon has raised her lamp above'.

Although he is hardly known today, George Macfarren was one of the mid-century's leading figures, producing comic operas (*Robin Hood, She stoops to conquer*), oratorios (*St John the Baptist* is the finest of these), symphonies, and chamber music. His series of Shakespeare settings, two of which are included here, shows an adventurous sense of texture and a spirited, fresh response to words. His younger brother, Walter, was also a noted composer.

In partsongs such as *Sweet and low* and *The long day closes* we find the epitome of what is understood by the term 'Victorian partsong'. Opinion seems divided as to their true musical worth, but of their genre they are both typical and perfect examples. Tennyson's cradle song could not be imagined in a more sympathetic setting, while Sullivan's music so far transcends the banality of Chorley's poem as to create a minor masterpiece. Many of Sullivan's Savoy operas contain partsongs or madrigals, but he composed a handful of separate pieces, two of which join *The long day closes* here as examples of his melodious art, brushed at auspicious moments by the delectable spirit of late-Victorian harmony.

In the music of Parry and Stanford we veer rapidly towards the Edwardian era and the enduring sense that 'ripeness is all'. Parry was a prolific composer—had he composed less, he might be more widely performed today. However, his reputation is sustained by such works as *Blest pair of sirens, Jerusalem,* some of the solo songs, and the *Songs of Farewell* (which might easily have been represented here, were there not other purely secular pieces with an equal claim). His style carries more than a trace of Brahms, filtered through the atmosphere of an English country house (ungenerous perhaps, but not entirely untrue), but at its best this music has passion, distinction, and the courage of its convictions. He also showed a discriminating taste in his choice of poetry, which included the Elizabethans and (as here) some of the finest nineteenth-century writing.

Also of a Brahmsian cast, especially in his church music, Stanford's is a refreshing voice with a deft sense of harmonic inflection. The impressionist tinges of *The blue bird* show a loosening of harmonic vocabulary which was soon to be extended by his contemporary Elgar, and the younger generation in the persons of Vaughan Williams and Delius.

With Elgar himself we reach an acknowledged master, although his partsongs can hardly be described as well-known today. They are, however, magnificent for their scale and, pleasingly, the texts chosen are generally of a high standard (certainly when compared with his solo songs).

Three of Elgar's younger contemporaries conclude this collection. Charles Wood was a prolific composer of church music (much of it still in use in our cathedrals) in which he tastefully indulges a passion for Tudor polyphony. He also wrote a successful madrigal, *If love be dead,* and his song *Ethiopia saluting the colours* remains an active member of the standard English song repertoire. The Scottish composer Hamish MacCunn was a keen follower of Wagner, and his opera *Jeanie Deans* (produced in Edinburgh in 1894) is probably his finest achievement. He was also the composer of some powerful, if ultimately rather derivative, songs and is perhaps at his best when the Scots influence is at its strongest, tempering the Wagnerian steel. Samuel Coleridge-Taylor's enduring monument, institutionalized by Sir Malcolm Sargent, is the cantata *Hiawatha's Wedding Feast.* He was of mixed West African and English descent, a heritage he explored in his *Bamboula Rhapsody,* the *African Romances* (songs), and the *Twenty-four Negro Melodies* for piano. From amongst a handful of partsongs, the chords of *Summer is gone,* piled high with thirds like a tall building perched on a landslide, seem a fitting conclusion to an anthology of romantic partsongs and, indeed, to an era.

If any final word in favour of English romantic partsongs were needed beyond the observation that they are rewarding to sing and to listen to, we might remember that music is a social activity before it is an object of cultural homage and critical evaluation. Today's art music, with only a few exceptions, is about as far removed from the general public as it could ever expect to be (though the general public is not too worried about this, of course). Music-making, as distinct from concert-going, played a far higher part in nineteenth-century domestic life than it does today. We have cause to reflect on this, and consider that in this vital respect at least, the Victorians still have something important to give us.

Paul Hillier
Rodmell, Sussex

1. O sing unto my roundelay

MADRIGAL

THOMAS CHATTERTON

SAMUEL WESLEY

2

6

2. Slow fresh fount

GLEE

BEN JONSON

11

3. Music, all powerful

GLEE

H. K. WHITE

THOMAS F. WALMISLEY

14

4. Home, sweet home

JOHN HOWARD PAYNE

HENRY BISHOP
Harmonized by T. CRAMPTON

5. Who shall have my lady fair

ANON.

ROBERT PEARSALL

26

6. Lay a garland

MADRIGAL

Words from Beaumont and Fletcher

ROBERT PEARSALL

Photocopying this copyright material is ILLEGAL.

32

7. Sir Patrick Spens

BALLAD-DIALOGUE

Traditional Scottish Ballad

ROBERT PEARSALL

36

38

* stormy

42

44

45

46

48

8. List! for the breeze

GLEE

Words from the Spanish

JOHN GOSS

50

9. Dirge for the faithful lover

BEAUMONT & FLETCHER

JULIUS BENEDICT

10. Stars of the summer night

HENRY LONGFELLOW

JOHN HATTON

58

sleeps!

sleeps!

sleeps!

sleeps!

2. Moon of the summer night!
   Far down yon western steeps,
   Sink, sink in silver light!
   She sleeps, my lady sleeps!

3. Wind of the summer night!
   Where yonder woodbine creeps,
   Fold, fold thy pinions light!
   She sleeps, my lady sleeps!

4. Dreams of the summer night!
   Tell her, her lover keeps watch!
   While in slumbers light!
   She sleeps, my lady sleeps!

11. An old romance

(*Drei Volkslieder*)

English text by
?Sabilla Novello

FELIX MENDELSSOHN
Op. 41 Nos. 2–4

PART I: O fly with me/*Entflieh' mit mir*

Un poco allegro

64

PART III: Over their grave /*Auf ihrem Grab*

66

12. Departure

Abschied vom Walde

JOSEPH VON EICHENDORFF
tr. W. BARTHOLOMEW

FELIX MENDELSSOHN
Op. 59 No. 3

68

70

13. Orpheus, with his lute

WILLIAM SHAKESPEARE

GEORGE MACFARREN

78

14. When daisies pied

WILLIAM SHAKESPEARE

GEORGE MACFARREN

82

15. Come live with me

CHRISTOPHER MARLOWE

WILLIAM STERNDALE BENNETT

90

16. Sweet Stream that winds through yonder glade

WILLIAM COWPER

WILLIAM STERNDALE BENNETT

17. Sweet and low

LULLABY

ALFRED, LORD TENNYSON

JOSEPH BARNBY

18. O hush thee, my babie

SIR WALTER SCOTT

ARTHUR SULLIVAN

Photocopying this copyright material is ILLEGAL.

19. Echoes

THOMAS MOORE

ARTHUR SULLIVAN

20. The long day closes

HENRY CHORLEY

ARTHUR SULLIVAN

* The small notes in the bass part are intended for use as *additional* notes, when the partsong is performed by a chorus.

© Oxford University Press 1986

Photocopying this copyright material is ILLEGAL.

21. There rolls the deep

ALFRED, LORD TENNYSON

C. HUBERT PARRY

22. Music, when soft voices die

PERCY BYSSHE SHELLEY

C. HUBERT PARRY

23. Heraclitus

WILLIAM CORY

CHARLES VILLIERS STANFORD
Op. 110 No. 4

Photocopying this copyright material is ILLEGAL.

24. The blue bird

MARY COLERIDGE

CHARLES VILLIERS STANFORD
Op. 119 No. 3

25. My love dwelt in a Northern land

ROMANCE

ANDREW LANG

EDWARD ELGAR
Op. 18 No. 3

* The passages of vocal accompaniment to be sung as softly and smoothly as possible and without accent.

26. As torrents in summer

HENRY LONGFELLOW

EDWARD ELGAR

27. Go, song of mine

GUIDO CAVALCANTI
tr. D. G. ROSETTI

EDWARD ELGAR
Op. 57

144

28. Full fathom five

WILLIAM SHAKESPEARE

CHARLES WOOD

29. Oh where art thou dreaming?

THOMAS MOORE

HAMISH MACCUNN

150

30. Summer is gone

CHRISTINA ROSSETTI

S. COLERIDGE-TAYLOR

156